DATE DUE

DATE DUE

MICHAEL JAMES
STUDIO QUILTS

Panorama: Konkordiaplatz 1, 1989
50" × 150" / 127 × 381 cm

Michael James wishes to dedicate this monograph to Donald Krueger, artist, teacher, and mentor, who opened doors to possibilities.

© 1995 Editions Victor Attinger SA
Avenue des Portes-Rouges 149, CH-2009 Neuchâtel, Switzerland

ISBN 2-88380-006-5
Library of Congress Catalog Card Number: 95-60086

Published and distributed in USA by:
Whetstone Hill Publications
P.O. Box 331
Swansea, Massachusetts 02777-0331
Phone: 508-324-4148   Fax: 508-676-8601

Printed in Switzerland

PATRICIA HARRIS AND DAVID LYON
PATRICIA MALARCHER

MICHAEL JAMES

STUDIO QUILTS

Michael James

ÉDITIONS VICTOR ATTINGER, NEUCHÂTEL
WHETSTONE HILL PUBLICATIONS, SWANSEA, MA.

nov. 14. 1995

Winter Cactus, 1978
42″×42″ / 107×107 cm

Yet the homier, domestic quilting tradition has a strong, emotional pull on James — as if he is always on the verge of revealing an organic form beneath the elegant geometry. The quilting world is dominated, for historical reasons, by values of the hearth, by emotional associations. In *Winter Cactus* we see the first of James' attempts to reconcile those domestic values and references to the natural world with the intellectual exploration of form, space and color. The title alone is a giveaway, but the shapes and colors likewise evoke the humble windowsill houseplant. At the same time, he is beginning the exploration of curved line by piling triangles upon trapezoids, approximating curve by the gradual reduction of angle.

Einstein's Space-Time: The Curved Plane

Around 1976, Michael James began to question the necessity of hand-piecing. Once he made the decision to machine-piece some quilts, his production sped up, and with it, his ability to experiment.

Yet the seminal quilt from this period, *Night Sky I* (1977), is not pieced at all: It is quilted on whole fabric. As such, it marks his most successful foray to that point into composing a quilt in a single unified field. The polished cotton, Prussian blue surface is meticulously quilted in a complex of swirled patterns (shades of van Gogh's *Starry Night*) that is richly evocative of its title subject, expressive of the artist's personality, and still exactingly geometric. This particular quilt simultaneously salutes the quilting tradition — such monochromatic *tours de force* of stitchery are a longstanding genre — and bids traditional quilting geometry adieu. The artist has subsumed the quilter.

The sequel, *Night Sky II* (1977), employs the stitchery forms in a pieced quilt with the edges of the pieces, in many cases, following the schematic laid out in *Night Sky I*. A couple of important steps occur at this stage. *Night Sky II* is the first of James' quilts to use strips of fabric — in this case, curved strips. Further, it marks the emergence of his interest in exploring color transitions and shadings — a very painterly problem made far more difficult in pieced cloth. It also marks the second in what would become a series of quilts with a theme of "air and light", as David Hornung puts it[4].

4 *Michael James*, by David Hornung. Essay in 10-year retrospective exhibition catalog. Worcester (Mass.) Craft Center, 1983.

Other quilts intervened, but James returned to the series of "sky" quilts, including *Aurora* (1978), *Moonshadow* (1979) and *Dawn Nebula* (1979). There is no denying that these three pieces form a gentle homage to the paintings of Sonia and Robert Delaunay, especially as they mirror in cloth some of their exploration of transparent color overlays while sharing an interest in the definition of space through interlocking curves. But keep in mind that James is working slowly and methodically in cloth, not quickly in paint, ink or any similarly fluid medium.

These three quilts that complete the sky suite also depart from the two *Night Sky* quilts in their approach to the celestial subject matter. *Night Sky I* is a rich evocation, as it were, of the *fabric* of space — the "ground" on which an earth-bound viewer sees the stars. *Night Sky II*, with its glimmers of color, suggests objects against that ground — objects that carve out the multi-dimensional nature of an otherwise flat perceptual ground. But *Aurora, Moonshadow* and *Dawn Nebula* do not take darkness and ground as their subject, but rather the transition between darkness and light. In *Aurora*, light itself is the figure, whereas in *Moonshadow* light is the ground and darkness is the figure. The complexity of *Dawn Nebula* makes reading the figure-ground relationship more difficult, but the artist triumphs over the limitations of cloth in a neo-Impressionist handling of brightness and hue transitions.

Inner Space: The Clockwork Rainbow

Having mastered the palette, Michael James' next seminal quilt was — again — a monochromatic piece with links both to the celestial series and a formal statement of the "next" world to conquer. *Suntreader: Monophony* (1979) is a logical progression in form and content, yet disturbingly different from earlier pieces.

The *Suntreader* series makes a clean break from the external grid while proclaiming the problem of the internal one. By dispensing with the rectangular nature of the quilt at a time when artists in various media were striving to "break the frame", James displays his intellectual affinity with the mainstream art problems of his time. But he also chooses to highlight the problem implicit in the quilt medium: the block. At the same time, he both mocks and does homage to the vanishing-point perspective of the Renaissance in the quilted lines. The "curve" converges with others like celestial railroad tracks disappearing in the infinity of space — or being consumed by the white fire of the sun. The nod to quilting tradition persists, of course, in *Suntreader: Monophony* — a stitchery manifesto tacked on the venerable door of the White Quilt.

The tension in this series grows directly from geometry as defined by frame (round), by stitch (curved and infinite), by block pattern (perpendicular), and, in *Suntreader No. 3* (1980), by color (diagonal or transverse). Coming as the pivotal series between the celestial images, which have fairly explicit references to the natural world, and the first of Michael James' strip-pieced construction quilts, which explicate Cartesian analytic geometry, the *Suntreader* quilts are simultaneously "of this world" and ethereal. They pronounce a formal theme of tension between the natural and the contrived — between the chaos of the phenomenological world and the pattern that the human mind contrives to give it order.

By the end of the 1970s, Michael James was working primarily in series of quilts, sometimes entirely in a single series, sometimes alternating between series. His next group — including *Quintet, Rhythmetron, Strip Quilt No. 5* and *Regatta* — marked a technical innovation that allowed James to explore color gradations in a more complex manner while still permitting visual "accidents" to occur in the studio. Because quilting is labor-intensive and slow, rarely does it allow for the happy accidents of painting, where a "mistake" opens up new possibilities.

But with this group James began to practice "strip-piecing". He would cut thin strips of colored fabric, then stitch them together in graduated hues or tones to create entirely new striped cloth. This "new" cloth would serve as the material for the quilt pieces. As a group, these quilts represent a transitional phase in James' work: a playful investigation of the possibilities of strip-piecing combined with a continued exploration of curved versus angular forms to define space and create a sense of movement. The resulting undulations suggest they could be known jointly as the "sine wave suite".

About 1981, James made a decision that has been controversial in some quarters: to sew entirely by machine. On one hand, it was a logical extension of his work to date. Strip-piecing virtually demanded the use of a sewing machine; as James observes, strip-piecing requires cutting across seams, and hand-sewn seams would tend to fall apart. And beginning with *Interweave*

Rhythmetron, 1981
68″×68″/173×173 cm

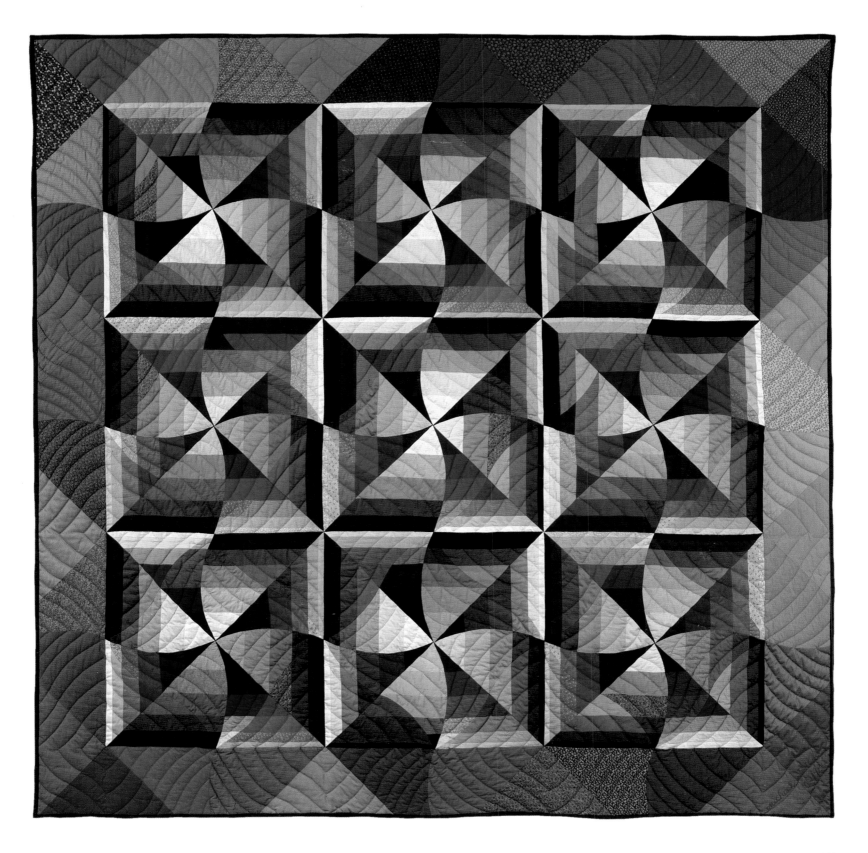

James decided to place his quilting "in the ditch", that is, in the seams between strips. This had the effect of making each piece more two-dimensional while de-emphasizing the three-dimensional "hand" of the cloth. It also made each piece less "quilt-like", if one considers decorative quilting an essential component of a traditional quilt. Admittedly, the argument about hand versus machine sewing was one of taste and identification with the handcraft tradition. James' hand-sewing was (and is) so meticulous that it is difficult to identify it as hand work. With the decision to minimize surface distraction, the necessity for handwork vanished.

By foregoing the contrast between a quilted surface and formal composition, James began to explore both the possibilities of color and brightness transitions inherent in strip-piecing and the geometric potentials of the technique. *Interweave II* (1982) recapitulates a theme from the celestial series — a bright central field that diminishes, like a sunset or an aurora, as it fades to darkness. The physical phenomenon of afterglow (or the halo effect of gravitational bending of light around massive bodies) seems to be at play here. The following sequence draws similarly on the natural world. *La Tempête* (1983) examines swirls of light playing, very much like a windstorm, through a stylized background of diagonal stripes and concentric diamond patterns — evocative of lightning. *Metamorphosis* (1983) and *Blue Undercurrents* (1984) feature many of the reciprocal wave forms of earlier series played against perpendicular stripes. By the time James concludes this series with *Air Structure* (1983) and *Air Structure 2* (1984), the intricacy of form that he has devised begins to hint of his later concern with shaped figures. But these worm-like stripes — reminiscent of the amoeboid forms of Joan Miró and Jean Arp — emerge from the strip-piecing. They are sine wave cuts from darker fabric on a light ground. With an aspect ratio of 1:3, the *Air Structure* quilts also depart radically from traditional quilt form. Their dimensions — 5 feet by 15 feet — echo their purpose as architectural installations in large spaces. (James' quilts are a good fit with contemporary architecture, as their crisp lines complement the relatively stripped-down line of most newer buildings while the colors and sensual qualities of the fabric soften an otherwise impersonal environment.)

Metamorphosis, 1984
84″×84″/213×213 cm

Zag-Edge 2, 1986
50″ × 50″ / 127 × 127 cm

18

Bidding the Grid Goodbye

In 1985, James began a series of quilts collectively called *Rhythm/Color* based on musical and dance motifs. A logical extension of the curvilinear diagonals that dominate the *Air Structure* quilts, they begin for the first time to employ curved forms that deliberately obscure the grid on which James had composed his quilts from the beginning. The grid is discernible as 10 × 10, but the quilts suggest certain dance forms that employ time signatures far more fluid than that regimented centennial metric. *Rhythm/Color: Spanish Dance* (1985) appears to use the sweepingly patterned areas of flamenco (in quartet form), while *Rhythm/Color: Morris Men* (1986) reflects the weaving pattern of that form of British folk dance. The references become less literal by the time James composed *Rhythm/Color: Bacchanal* (1986), with its whirling figures and complex geometry of nine circles on the 10 × 10 grid [5]. *Rhythm/Color: Improvisation 3* (1987) has left the comparatively simple rhythmic figures of folk dance behind in favor of a wave-like progression from jazz. Notably, this is a rare composition in that it "moves" from lower right to upper left.

Following the *Rhythm/Color* series, James began to work with radical angles in the *Zag* suite that includes *Zag-Edge*, *Zag-Edge 2* and *Bias Cut* (all 1986). These particular quilts employ the illusion of spatial planes to disguise the grid, almost obliterating it. A close examination of each quilt shows the 10 × 10 grid (including the single-block "border"), but the complexity of composition distracts the eye from that formal arrangement. Strong diagonals play a part in the illusion, but the juxtaposition of differing brightness levels determines the apparent planes.

Immediately following, James began to synthesize the lessons of the *Rhythm/Color* and *Zag* series with a small suite illustrated here by *Red Zinger* (1986) and *Window Piece* (1987). In effect, they merge the diagonals of the *Zag* quilts with the curves of the *Rhythm/Color* pieces. In addition, they deliberately violate the frame with small segments that project beyond their box-like enclosures. The grid on which they are composed has all but vanished. In a postscript to this stage of dismantling the grid, James constructed *Neo-Geo* in 1987 — a series of cloth panels (some strip-pieced, some

---

5 Perhaps the inspiration had something to do with the greater abstraction. James modeled the *Bacchanale* sequence on Saint-Saen's *Samson et Dalila*.

not) in three dimensions. Certain panels actually overlap the others, and the grid has no traces at the surface. Notably, this quilt parallels a style favored by many artists working in craft media in the late 1980s, including wood, glass and jewelry. It is a post-modernist pop style, evanescent in its popularity and unique in James' work.

The radical forms of *Neo-Geo* find an analog, however, in *Flying Buttress* (1988), a quilt that employs James' exploration of the tension between angled and curved forms. Part of what is notable about this quilt in the context of James' development is that the figure appears to float in space, not on a ground per se. In this manner it prefigures a series of quilts later in 1988 that break the smooth edges of the frame completely.

Double Image and *Rain Dance* (both 1988) continue James' exploration of planar levels with a tension between curved and straight diagonals. The "forms", if one can call them that, appear to extend beyond the limits of the quilt edges into an imaginary infinity, defined both by light-like rays and wave-like ripples. In *Split Shift* (1988), the frame is divided diagonally with angular forms on the upper left, curved forms on the lower right, prefiguring the Cascade series.

The *Cascade* quilts include *Cascade: Double Diagonal, Cascade 4, Red/Green Cascade* and *Double Cascade: Yang, Yin.* Superficially, they read as rippling waves superimposed on square planes within square planes. The sense of continuity beyond the frame is again strong, implying the passage of time from memory (outside the frame) to present (the "snapshot" depicted) to future. Their very simplicity and insistency imply a continuity of phenomena and, hence, of experience. That which was, is and will be.

The *Waves* series, shown here as *Waves 1, Waves 2: Storm Surge* and *Waves III,* picks up some of these same concerns more literally with the concept of water as a form. But two notable changes also appear: the introduction of entire planes that wave and swirl instead of just lines, and the willingness to abandon the continuous line of the traditional quilt. James' previous quilts were largely square or rectangular, although he also made a few circular quilts. In either case, however, the integrity of the continuous frame held. The *Waves* series, however, violates that line to create a vivid sense of movement, as if the waveforms are rolling across the flat plane of an ocean surface.

A contemporaneous group of quilts, the *Shadowbox* series, plays with the opposition of triangular forms with a strong diagonal thrust. Represented here

Split Shift, 1988
43"×51"/109×130 cm

by *Transparent Shadowbox* (1988), *Point/Counterpoint* (1989), and *Zed Structure* (1990), this series shows James examining ways to redivide the "box" of the quilt surface by transecting it. Thus, the receding planes of ever-smaller box-like structures contend with the diagonal transects to create a vigorous — and shifting — perspective.

By 1989, Michael James has succeeded in entirely obscuring the grid structure beneath his quilt compositions, creating a fabric art in some ways analogous to monumental abstraction in painting, albeit with somewhat different

Aletsch, 1990
41"×83"/104×211 cm
Museum of the American Quilter's Society, Paducah, Kentucky

concerns imposed by the quilt medium and the cultural/artistic history of quilting.

With the *Konkordiaplatz* group (1989-1990), which includes *From the Mountaintop, Panorama: Konkordiaplatz 1* and *2,* and *Aletsch*, James draws from the natural world. As he says, "These quilts represent efforts to synthesize my sensory responses to a particular space: the vast mountainous basin in the Swiss Alps that encloses the Aletsch glacier, the largest in Europe. In the summer of 1988 I spent several days hiking along its perimeter, which extends many kilometers from the Jungfrau firn. What impressed me most was the very audible sound of millions of gallons of water rushing unseen beneath the perfectly still expanse of glacier. It seemed incongruous: the unrelenting movement of so much water and the stony rigidity of so much ice."

What a marvelous analogy to his own work! A strong, if sometimes hidden, affinity for the natural world runs through Michael James' quilt compositions, and the Aletsch glacier was a perfect metaphor for his struggle between solid, uncollapsing forms and liquidity of movement.

The lessons of the *Konkordiaplatz* group reverberate in the quilts that immediately follow, notably *Sky/Wind Variations* (1990), *Sky/Wind Variations 2* (1990) and *Expanded Force Field* (1991). The composition of *Sky/Wind Variations* in four individual panels both echoes the altar-screen references of the *Konkordiaplatz* group, and the four winds/four directions tradition of a more naturistic creed. At the same time, James is also exploring further the compositional ramifications of waveforms — notably the interlock of crest and trough. *Expanded Force Field* examines energy from the other perspective — the particle instead of the wave. While on one hand the composition might be seen as harnessing vectors, it also represents an interesting play of form versus color. Although the composition can be dissected as a series of interlocking right triangles, color leads the eye away from closure of the form, creating a dynamic that literally explodes, i. e., forcefully expands toward and, by implication, beyond the frame.

Making Idylls With Feet of Klee

Expanded Force Field represents a solution in James' work, at least for the time being, to handling angular forms. In 1992, he began a series that fuses his sophistication in representing curved forms and his elegant formalism with angles. *Bourrée*, the first of the group, limited the variations in curves to concentrate on working out the fusions of color from area to area; as such it is the curvilinear counterpart to *Expanded Force Field*. The title, James says, comes from a movement of Bach's third solo cello suite, and the interplay of form and tonality certainly suggests both the intricate formality of Bach and the mellow timbre of the cello.

In this series, James has let go entirely of the grid structure without calling attention to that achievement. (It is possible to superimpose a grid on many of these compositions, just as it is possible in analytical geometry to describe any curve. But a grid analysis is exactly that — an imposition, not a master plan.) Finding his way to freedom from geometry also seems to have sparked an intensely fertile period.

Lush Life is something of a turning point, since it both looks backward to James' fondness for biomorphic forms and forward to an individual geometric vocabulary. A kind of joy seems to spring from the surface, as vigorous (and

Bourrée, 1992
47″×47″ / 119×119 cm

vegetative) forms exude an animal energy. The companion piece, *Hot Pursuit*, shares the vigor and the biomorphism. Surface overpowers structure, redefining a space that becomes all the more intimate for its lack of grid-structure monumentality. Note as well, some of the forms that look back to the pointed curves of Asian landscapes/seascapes — the cresting waves of Japanese prints, the bamboo of Chinese brush paintings. The orientalism is hardly a coincidence. *Processional* formalizes movement in direct reference to traditional Japanese court dance and pantomime.

At the same time, Michael James the ascetic has an obverse: Michael James the sybarite. The forms of *Suspended Animation* directly echo those of *Processional*, but they are composed in a radically different way. Whereas *Processional* marches across the frame in stately fashion, the curved and jagged forms of *Suspended Animation* form a dervish-like maelstrom of activity. James has said that he sought to reproduce the "spontaneity of graffiti" with this work. He accomplished his goal.

The title of *Suspended Animation* is a clue to James' intent in this series of post-grid quilts. The activity seems suspended indeed — a snapshot of intricate dance-like movement. Compare the successor quilt, *Electric Boogie* (1993), which plays with comparable forms but which, by using a brighter ground and greater contrast, creates the illusion of active rather than captive movement. *Electric Boogie* also draws the eye beyond the individual forms to a consideration of rhythms denoted with bright patches in the upper left and lower right, separated by a diagonal band from lower left to upper right. The off-center brightness of the corner patches suggests the syncopation within a 4/4 timeframe — an apt representation of boogie's treatment of measure and rhythm.

If there's one lesson in looking at Michael James' career, however, it is that neither an Apollonian nor a Dionysian impulse dominates for long. In *Vortex* (1993) he returns to an emphasis on ovoid forms, piled up in layers of space in transects of an inverted cone. In contrast to the activity implicit in the title, this quilt conveys a tranquility and solidity, achieved in part by a subdued palette.

Formalism appears even more explicitly in *Quilt No. 150 (Rehoboth Meander)* (1993) through an ordered arrangement of four columns and an exploration of James' peculiar forms as stand-ins for ideographs. Suggestive of columnar writing, it begs the question of meaning by appearing at once representational of script and simultaneously entirely self-referential in its symbols. The subsequent rectangular quilt *Out of Line* (1994) tumbles the forms, suggesting that the pair might be thought of as a duet — a before and after of meaning, or the monument and its equally beautiful ruins.

Between the two, James revisits his comb-like forms in *Full Circle* (1993), one of two quilts that return to the circle for a different series of explorations than those in the *Suntreader* series a decade and a half earlier. *Full Circle* is what might be called an inhabited world — an active colony of forms swimming in close harmony beneath a circular membrane. *Roundabout* (1994), on the other hand, gracefully combines the curved and triangular forms to suggest a convex view of the skin of the sphere.

Although the quilts of 1992-94 hardly represent a conclusion of Michael James' career, they do capture the artist at a promontory of mastery. He has effectively solved certain apparent limitations of the quilt form as an artistic medium — specifically the grid — and has, for a while, settled the conflict between lyric spontaneity and a rage for order. Rich in color, dynamic in form, playful in conception, they represent an artist who has fashioned a new order for his medium — the exploding joy of brushwork expressed with the modestly subordinated labor of pieced cloth.

Patricia Harris and David Lyon

Meadow Lily, 1974
84″×84″/213×213 cm

28

Elabored Tangram, 1976
94″×94″/239×239 cm

Bedloe's Island Pavement, 1975
84″ × 76″ / 213 × 193 cm

31

Suntreader No 3, 1980
⌀60" / ⌀152 cm

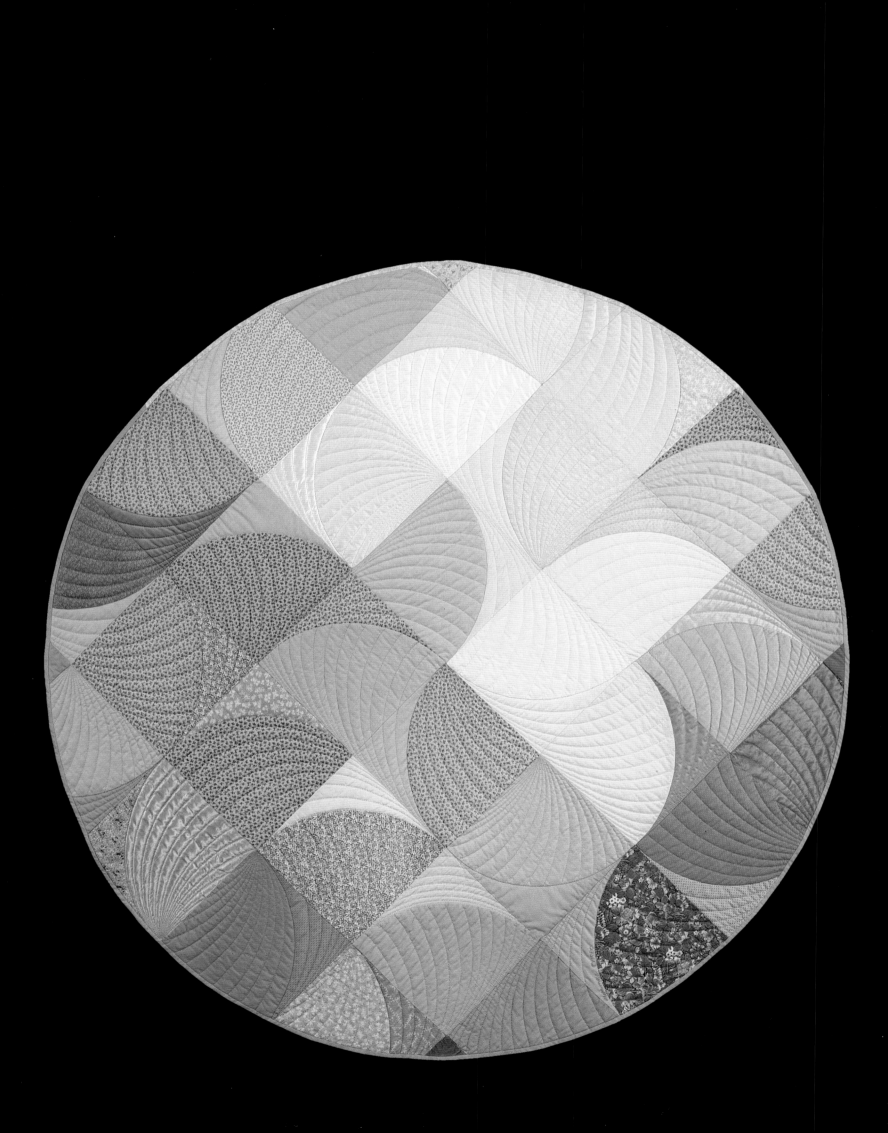

La Tempête, 1983
87″ × 79″ / 221 × 201 cm

38

Blue Undercurrents, 1983
70″ × 70″ / 178 × 178 cm

Air Structure, 1983
60″×180″/152×457 cm

Air Structure 2: Three Brightly Colored Squares, 1984
58″ × 174″ / 147 × 442 cm

Rhythm/Color: Spanish Dance, 1985
100″×100″ / 254×254 cm
The Newark Museum, Newark, New Jersey

Rhythm/Color: Morris Men, 1986
100″×100″ / 254×254 cm

Bias Cut, 1986
67″×88″ / 170×224 cm

Red Zinger, 1986
67″×69″/170×175 cm

Flying Buttress, 1988   ▷
49″×103″/124×262 cm

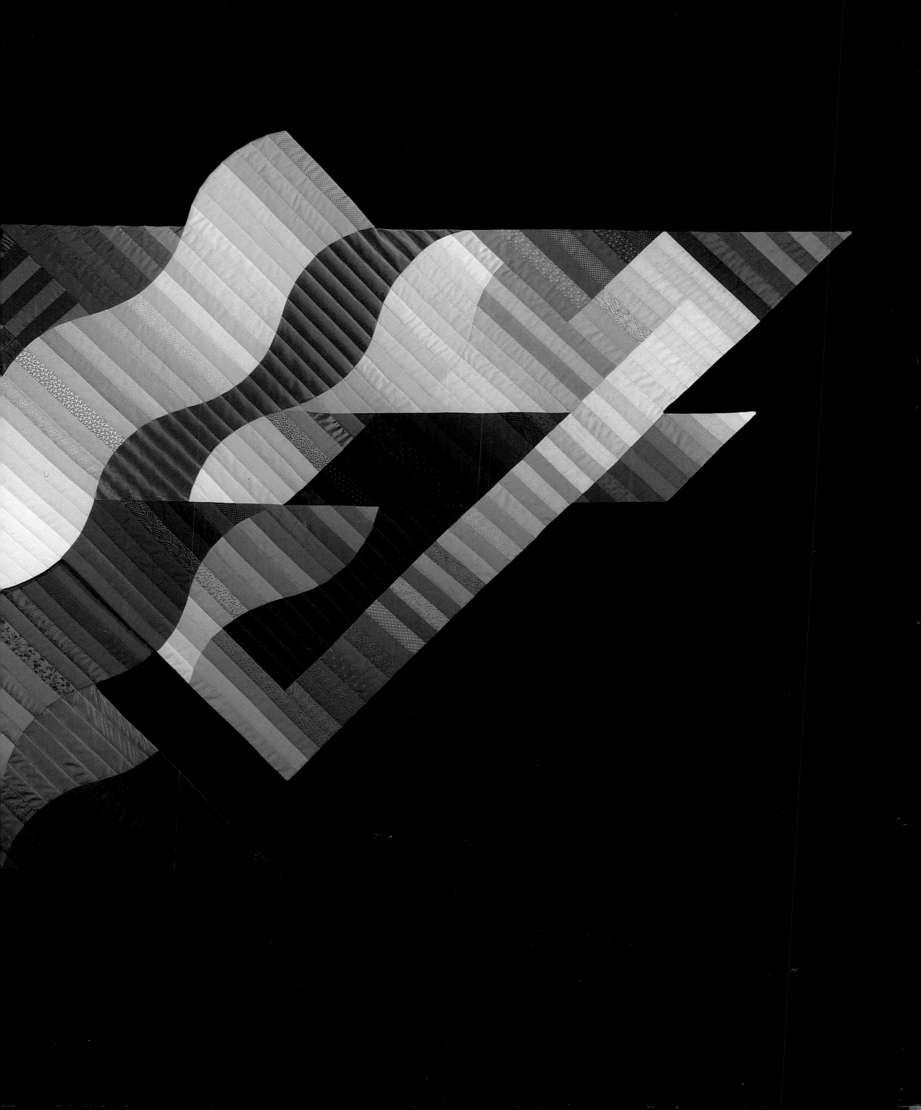

◁ *Double Image*, 1987
108"×72"/274×183 cm

Rain Dance, 1987
57"×57"/145×145 cm
Ulster Folk and Transport Museum, Belfast, North Ireland

Cascade: Double Diagonal, 1988
57″ × 57″ / 145 × 145 cm

Cascade 4, 1989
45″×45″/114×114 cm

Double Cascade: Yang, Yin, 1989
51″×102″/130×259 cm

Waves 1, 1988
84″×98″/213×249 cm

Transparent Shadowbox, 1988
56″ × 56″ / 142 × 142 cm

Expanded Force Field, 1991
79″ × 79″ / 201 × 201 cm

From the Mountaintop, 1989
68″ × 90½″ / 173 × 230 cm

Sky/Wind Variations, 1990
72″×144″/183×366 cm

76

Lush Life, 1992
73″×73″/185×185 cm

Suspended Animation, 1992
90″ × 90″ / 229 × 229 cm

Quilt N° 150 (Rehoboth Meander), 1993
53" × 53½" / 135 × 136 cm
The Renwick Gallery of the National Museum of American Art,
Smithsonian Institution, Washington, D.C.

Full Circle, 1993
⌀67½″ / ⌀171 cm

Roundabout 1994
⌀77" / ⌀196 cm

Out of Line, 1994
45½″ × 45½″ / 116 × 116 cm

The Metaphysics of Action (Entropic Forms), 1994
101″×101″/257×257 cm

Michael James: an Interview

Patricia Malarcher: How did you come to realize that, in quilts, you had found your own voice?

Michael James: It was a gradual process. To be honest, it seems that it's only in the last six or seven years that I've found it. The first thirteen of fourteen years were really a period of searching after who I was artistically. I did know, early on, that it was with quilts that I wanted to develop a life's work, because there I had found a marriage of me and the materials more compelling than with paint and brushes and canvas.

PM: Would you speak about the difference between making quilts and working with paint?

MJ: There are huge differences. The primary one is the insistent, process-oriented, step-by-step nature of building a quilt, starting with pieces A and B and building on those systematically, doing certain things in a certain order. In painting you can put diverse materials together in random order and build in a less constrained way. I related better to an orderly kind of construction than to the open-ended possibilities that working on a canvas offered.

PM: The way you describe it, your work seems allied to architecture.

MJ: For a while, I considered the possibility of studying architecture, but I went into painting because something in me sought the kind of freedom that painting represents. Despite the limitations I've described in relation to quilts, I have experienced a sense of liberation — an experience that a painter might identify with — in making them. I feel that I've been able to rise over those limitations, and that it's been an exciting challenge to do so.

PM: Looking at slides of your work, from the earliest to the most recent pieces, I was aware of a progression from a unit-by-unit construction in an obvious grid to compositions with an overall flow that seem to reclaim the space of a painter.

MJ: I think I made a breakthrough a couple of years ago, one that I'd been aiming toward for seven or eight years, allowing me to leave

Zag-Edge 2, 1986
50" × 50" / 127 × 127 cm

behind the understructure. The traditional notion of what a quilt was had imposed the grid on my work as it has on that of most people making quilts over the last twenty years. At first I was comfortable with the grid, and it served my purposes, but I got to the point where I began to see it as a kind of prison. It became a necessity to break away from it. Then I did a series in which, although you couldn't see a literal grid on the surface, there was an underlying grid that supported what was on the surface. Finally, two years ago I eliminated the underlying grid; that opened up a huge range of possibilities.

PM: Did that breakthrough happen during your residency at the Chateau de La Napoule?

MJ: It was definitely tied to having had the residency, because it was there that I went back to working on paper and working primarily with oil-based pastels and crayons for the first time in nearly twenty years. That way of working was so different from the processes in which I had immersed myself; it reminded me that there was a whole other way of working and creating images. My focus had been so concentrated that I hadn't allowed room for that kind of experimentation. It also reminded me of the importance of play, especially play with unconventional materials or with materials that aren't the stuff with which an artist usually works. Out of that period came a number of drawings which, although not quilt-like, embodied images that I eventually recognized as relevant to the types of fabric surfaces that I'd been creating. I started a series of quilts in 1992 whose roots are in several of those drawings; they were the first that completely abandoned the underlying grid.

PM: In choosing the quilt as your form of expression, did you consider that you would have to confront different issues surrounding the work such as the question of art versus craft, or the fact of being a minority male in a dominantly female world?

MJ: I certainly thought of both of those things. As for the question of art versus craft, I'll say that for myself personally, it's never been an issue. I see many quilts, including some of my own, that are fully as artful as many paintings, sculptures, or objects that one would regard as conventional fine art forms. The work of one's hands and mind in producing an object is the same from medium to medium. I don't think there's a significant difference, although there might be a difference in terms of intent.

PM: What do you mean?

MJ: Well, if I decide to make a quilt, and open a book to look for a pattern, and decide to make a Bear's Paw pattern for my queen-size bed, and end up with an object that is 90 inches by 100 inches and drapes well over the sides of the bed and covers the pillows when the bed is made and provides warmth at night when the bed isn't made, and provides decorative interest to the room by virtue of its pattern, and is the result of hundreds of hours of careful stitching and attention to process, I don't think I've necessarily created a work of art.

PM: What have you created?

MJ: I've created a bed quilt, an object for use. Now if I decide to make a quilt that's 90 by 100 inches, and is a configuration of forms and colors, materials and techniques which, as a whole, give realization to some image that comes out of my own experience and thought processes and feelings about art and design and pattern as well as the notion of what quilts are or have been or can be, and that may work on a bed but doesn't have to in order to be understood, the odds are better that I will have produced something that might be considered art. I may not do that every time, but that's true of any artist.

PM: Could you define the difference between art, craft, and design?

MJ: Art is a state, a situation that a work enters when its expressive, symbolic, metaphorical, and/or decorative value assumes a communicative power that transcends its materiality. To me, craft is the process, the construction, the technical aspect of producing some object. To a degree, design is technical also, but whereas craft is focused on the construction end of the object, design is focused on the composition — essentially, on the interweaving of the surface elements — line, color, form, shape, etc.

PM: Would you say that design is concerned with both functional and aesthetic ends?

MJ: Yes, depending on what you're designing. If you're designing a piece of furniture, you have to be concerned about functional aspects. But you don't have to think functionally in terms of quilts, at least not in regard to studio quilts or art quilts. Most of them are thought of in the same terms as a painting: something to go on a wall, with a decorative or communicative purpose — that is its function.

PM: But what is it that pushes good design and good craft into art?

MJ: All I can say is that there's something intangible embodied in a work of art that has the capacity to draw emotional and psychological responses from someone who encounters it. Most objects that are purely functional don't have that intangible quality.

Razzle Dazzle, 1975
96"×84"/244×213 cm

PM: Beyond craftsmanship and design, art today is regarded as something that holds a mirror up to a particular culture and talks back to it in ways that are often confrontational. Where do you see your work in such a milieu?

MJ: I don't see that my work really fits in with what's going on in the art world today. It seems to fit in with what is going on in the studio craft movement. What I've said regarding quilts could be said about any studio craft medium like glass, furniture, ceramics, or other textiles. None of those really fit in with the currents of avant-garde art.

PM: Is the choice of making work that is harmonious rather than disturbing an escape from the real world?

MJ: When I'm in my studio I don't think in those terms but I can say this about my work: I'm by nature a very ordered person who depends on and likes a fair amount of structure in my life. Perhaps one reason I turned to quilts is because of the order that is imposed on process. The type of quilts that I make is a reflection of the type of person I am. That brings to mind the issue of stripes. I've been working with stripes for the last twelve or thirteen years. There's something about the regularity and the consistency that appeals to me, that I relate to, that gives me pleasure and satisfaction. Stripes are universal and elemental forms, archetypes in a way.

PM: Do you feel that by creating stripes in a physical way from fabric rather than by drawing or painting them on a surface, you are asserting their essence more emphatically?

MJ: Exactly. I'm not just making a flattened representation of a stripe, but I'm actually cutting the stripe and then putting many of these stripes together to make panels that become multicolored strip surfaces or expanses. It's a lot more labor-intensive to cut and sew stripes than it is to paint stripes. But it's never crossed my mind to paint the images I'm doing in fabric. If I were going to paint I would do something else.

PM: Although you might use a hundred fifty colors in the stripes of a quilt, there is a certain quality of light in your color that is uniquely yours. Is that intended?

MJ: When I'm doing the construction of the strip panels, which is a prelude to the actual creation of a quilt surface, I first choose the colors of fabric which will later be cut up into strips and then sewn into large panels. I choose 36 colors, on average, for each panel, usually without a particular reference to anything external to the color itself. I do decide occasionally, when I'm running low on

94

them, that I need to make very light runs of color in my panels, or runs that are warm or bluish or whatever. This is not done with any thought of creating a particular light effect later, but to fill in a gap in the color palette. Obviously, in a lot of my work the issue of light and space has been a concern and in composing many pieces I deliberately focused on them. But that was an afterword, if you will, to the composition of the stripes themselves.

PM: After you've made these panels and put a piece together, do you ever have a sense of connecting with something outside the work?

MJ: Sometimes when I start composing a piece on the wall I start to make associations with some natural or emotional reference, but my work is essentially abstract. There's very little in the whole body of my work that could be construed as representational although there are some pieces that have a representational aspect.

PM: What about the shapes suggestive of biomorphic forms in your newest pieces?

MJ: I can't say that I went about looking for biomorphic forms, but the forms that started to happen had a biomorphic quality. I make a particular shape, and step back and think, 'Oh, that shape looks like a leaf, or is starting to look like a flower or whatever.' It's not done with any intent, but is the shape that results from an effort to organize the space of the surface. It's an intuitive way to work, and is not often governed by some fixed idea of what I want to express or represent.

PM: Let's go back to your being among a male minority in the quilt field.

MJ: I did wonder, when I first got involved in quilts, what people would think of a man getting this serious and this focused on something that men, except for a handful, simply didn't do. I came to the conclusion that I had to do what I felt would feed me regardless of what anybody thought.

PM: Has being in a minority been advantageous?

MJ: Any minority attracts a certain amount of attention as a novelty, but I have always felt that the novelty of my gender in this medium wasn't enough to sustain interest in my work — the work itself had to speak and its construction had to be as rock-solid as any around. I think that has had more to do with the response that my work has received than the fact that I'm a man doing it. With all the discussion and theorizing that's gone on about gender roles in recent

Tossed Salad Quilt, 1976
102" × 90" / 259 × 229 cm

years, including the push against the dominant white male in contemporary society, I have felt somewhat uncomfortable when I've been put in a position of authority. I've juried shows, written catalogues, reviewed shows and books and so on related to the quilt world. So by virtue of my straight, conventional, late 1960s — early 1970s fine arts education, I could be perceived as a white male 'establishment' voice in a field that is 99% female. Certainly, some individuals are hostile to that male voice. Yet, I feel that my convictions about the validity of this medium relative to other media is proof of my commitment to quilts and quiltmaking and quiltmakers.

PM: Let's shift gears. You've mentioned Charles Sheeler as an influence; how is this reflected in your work?

MJ: I've been a longtime admirer of Charles Sheeler and a number of other Precisionist painters of the 1920s and 1930s, but I can't say they've actually influenced my work. Certainly, I've been attracted to that type of work, and have drawn from it an analogy with the type of work that I do, because I see it as precisionist.

PM: It's often said that people in craft mediums tend to take ideas that have already been developed in other fields, and simply rework them in different materials. It seems that when Sheeler and his contemporaries were working, there was a general interest in the phenomenon of light and they were expressing this in paint. Today, that's not a primary interest in painting, but your work still seems to reflect it. How would you answer someone who saw in your work a recycling of someone else's color theory into your own materials?

MJ: At this point, I don't think that my own way of handling color and of dealing with light and space and so on is derivative of any particular artist or style. If I were to feel that everything I did was derivative, then there'd be no reason to do it. But I have to admit that I feel a lot of what's going on in studio crafts, particularly in studio quilts, has been done before.

PM: Let's talk more about these images coming into your work. They seem ambiguous, rather than specific. Do you think of them as metaphorical?

MJ: The free-form images I'm currently working with were foreshadowed by the drawings that I did in the fall of 1990, but when I did them I had no idea in mind of what I wanted them to represent.

PM: Were you drawing from nature, or imagination?

MJ: I was drawing out of experience, and I was using drawing, as I use the designing of my quilt surfaces, as a way to swim in the world of color and form, to revel in the beauty of pure color and pure form. Essentially it's a reflection of an Abstract Expressionist approach to surface design. And, saying that, I realize that it's passé in relation to how people are thinking about artmaking today.

PM: You've spoken of having been trained in an Abstract Expressionist mode. Are there particular artists from the Abstract Expressionist school that have influenced you?

MJ: Are you asking whether my imagery reflects elements in other artists' work?

PM: Not necessarily; one can also be influenced by an artist's philosophy or an idea about what art is.

MJ: In that case I would say that hundreds of artists have influenced my work. I have made a point to learn about artists' lives through biographies or autobiographies, as well as artists' writings and commentaries on their work or on movements they've been involved in, and so on. When an observer discusses my work, he'll often see the influence of Frank Stella — his name comes up a lot, of course, because in the 60s Stella was doing the stripes and the compass curves and the protractor series. But from my vantage point, those have been the least influential among Stella's works; what have had more of an impact on me have been the aluminum, free-form constructions. Maybe in those there was a clue to understanding how I could develop form that would go beyond the grid substructure. I've looked at a lot of work by artists who would be thought of as colorists. David Hockney comes to mind. I don't look at my work and think of David Hockney, and I don't think many people would, but I think that his work has influenced mine. Matisse is another, but of course Matisse influenced Hockney, as Picasso did. The question of influences is very complex.

PM: Sometimes, influence can be subliminal, unrecognized until a work is completed.

MJ: Well, the range of artists that I've looked at and absorbed through their work goes from the people we just spoke about to people like Bridget Riley, Francis Bacon, Brice Marden, Frida Kahlo, Andy Goldsworthy — I'm naming artists whose work is very divergent and who cover a broad range of styles, just to make the point. My work has also been influenced by my study of Amish quilts and other textiles including African fabrics and Central and South American weaving. And I don't want to overlook the influence that the work of other studio craft artists has had on my own. The glass artist, Dale Chihuly, for example, and Diane Itter, who made absolutely incredible hand-knotted constructions, have both affected my work.

Suntreader Monophony, 1979
⌀60" / ⌀152 cm
Ball State University Gallery of Art, Muncie, Indiana

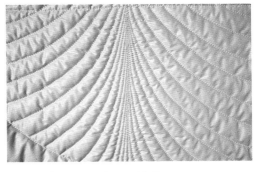

Suntreader Monophony, 1979
Detail view/Détail

PM: What about artists who focused on color, like Josef Albers or Richard Anuszkiewicz?

MJ: Anyone who went through art school in the 60s studied Albers so I'm certainly cognizant of everything he stood for. So yes, Albers has influenced my work, as well as Anuszkiewicz and the color op art stuff of the 60s and 70s. But what's influenced me more than their actual pieces has been what these people have said about their work.

PM: Could you give an example?

MJ: Well, for instance, Bridget Riley, in a catalogue essay, spoke about light and space and seeking a way to give visual form to an experience of a particular type of light at a particular moment of the day under particular climatic conditions. That idea speaks to me in a way that some of her paintings don't; perhaps she didn't succeed at doing what she set out to do because it was so elusive.

PM: Could you cite another example?

MJ: Well, there's Frida Kahlo, but again it's less a matter of the work itself being an influence. With her, it's a way of approaching the world, of being, in terms of the world. It's a sense of utter honesty and a kind of self-assuredness and self-awareness in the face of a large measure of — how do I express it? — inadequate attention.

PM: Do you mean that she knew she was a better artist than people gave her credit for being?

MJ: Exactly, and the fact that she knew that she wasn't getting the attention she deserved didn't dissuade her in any way. She continued, despite great odds, to do what she knew she had to do. That's the type of thing that will influence me. It's what motivates me to continue doing what I do.

PM: How do you view the critically acclaimed fabric works of Lucas Samaras?

MJ: I was really energized by those fabric constructions he did back in the late 70s and early 80s. I came to New York to see those pieces in shows at the Pace Gallery and I also saw a collection at the Chicago Art Institute. Hilton Kramer did a long review of those pieces in the New York Times. He made reference to a resurgence of interest in patchwork and quilts but said Samaras was the only person to do anything original with it. Looking back, I think I now agree with him although I didn't then. However, I think that since then original work has been done in the fabric medium by people

Quintet, 1980
68″×68″ / 173×173 cm

who weren't tied into the New York art world. I actually saw Samaras' things more as paintings than as quilts. In fact, they were pieced fabric constructions that were stretched on stretcher frames; he never pretended to be making quilts.

PM: Today, a big issue in the art world is the intellectual content in the work. Would you say that, for you, the content is in the formal qualities?

MJ: There's no doubt that it's largely in the formal qualities. I've chosen not to put any kind of weighty sociological message in my work. It's just not what the work is about, and I'll never pretend that it is.

PM: Do you have a weighty philosophical reason for not doing so?

MJ: I suppose it's partly an impulse that has always been strong not to jump on the bandwagon; I haven't felt the need to. I've looked at the world, let's say, with a sense of awe. I've been attracted by what is harmonious and what is beautiful in the physical world, and I think my work has always been an attempt to synthesize my response to that. Now, certainly if I walk out the door of this building onto West 23rd St., within a block I'm going to encounter half a dozen homeless people begging for money. It's outrageous that our society is incapable of providing its inhabitants with the things they need. But I don't feel any impulse to go back to my studio and make a quilt about homelessness or about societal inequities or injustices. It's not that I think that type of work can't be important and compelling — some of it is — but it's not what I'm interested in reflecting in my work.

PM: Could it be that in committing yourself to that which is harmonious and orderly, qualities which may have a kind of soothing value that is lacking in the world at large, you are helping to introduce or inject a sort of balance into the world?

MJ: I know this is true because people have told me that my work gives them a means to escape the oppressive realities that surround most of us on a daily basis. In that sense, my quilts function as metaphors for a perfect world. That's what they are for me. I can't control the world around me, but I can control color and form and fabric in my work; it's my only means of approaching perfection or harmony.

PM: Let's go back to your use of stripes, which you called "archetypal". Since archetypes are rooted in universal human experience, could you relate the striped structure to some specific kind of experience?

Regatta, 1981
52″ × 52″ / 132 × 132 cm

MJ: Ultimately, I see the stripe as a kind of timeline. A stripe for me is like the line of somebody's life.

PM: Do you mean that it represents continuity?

MJ: I guess it's a symbol for order; I think that searching after order is an elemental drive even though nature may seem to conspire against that. It's also the elemental, rhythmic patterning, the plus and minus, yin and yang quality to the composition of a field of stripes that appeals to me.

PM: Your reference to rhythmic patterning reminds me of something we haven't yet talked about: you once mentioned that music has been important in the development of your work.

Neo-Geo, 1987
43″ × 58″ / 109 × 147 cm

MJ: I work in my studio with music as a complement to whatever I'm doing. I know that when I'm building a piece on the wall and making decisions about forms and colors and placement and tensions and movements and all of that, I'm subconsciously reacting to the music that I'm hearing or that I've been listening to in the days or weeks leading up to that particular work. So, while the rhythms in the pieces are visual, they also are based on musical rhythms which by some sort of osmosis work their way into the quilts. I've always felt that visual surfaces could function as analogs to particular pieces of music; when I'm thinking about things that are happening in the surface of a quilt, I think of terms like timbre and brilliance and dissonance. I think of a run of colors or an interplay of colored stripes in a particular sequence as a segue from one area to another, or as an arpeggio or whatever, depending on what's going on.

PM: You were speaking of Frida Kahlo, and the fact that you could empathize with her persistence in spite of inadequate attention. Yet, you yourself have attained a level of success that, among artists, is above the average. You've been able to survive on your art, to support a family, to travel.

MJ: You talk about a certain measure of success and recognition but that has been in a fairly small arena. The quilt world itself is a pond, and that is where most of my recognition has come from. The craft world, the fine craft world, is a small lake perhaps, and a certain measure of recognition has come from there. Then there's the ocean, certainly the great lake, that is the art world, and where does what I do fit into that?

PM: Does that bother you?

MJ: No, it doesn't bother me. I hope that a hundred years from now some of this work will still have the capacity to affect someone, but that's not why I'm doing it.

PM: At this point in your career, are you aware of any acquired wisdom, or insight, realized through the process of working?

MJ: I guess it would be that ultimately you're the only person that you have to answer to. If you respond to others rather than responding to yourself, the idea of producing work with integrity will remain elusive; you'll never do it. The only way you can produce work that has integrity is by turning inward and acknowledging the truth of who you are as a person and of establishing what your relationship to the process of artmaking is, or what you want it to be, and then working toward that. Despite what anyone else brings to your work you're the ultimate judge, and you have to be loyal to that inner voice that is the best guide that you're likely to have. Certainly other people can help, but other people can also trip you up. So finally you answer to yourself, and I think ultimately that's where integrity comes from. "Know thyself" — it sounds simplistic, but essentially that's what it is.

Patricia Malarcher

Michael James at work

Fabrics for a new strip panel are selected from the artist's stock and arranged in varied groupings based on color, value, or intensity contrasts and usually representing graded runs that form a natural sequence.

Once a grouping of 36 fabrics is chosen and arranged to complete a strip panel, it is divided into groups of 9 fabrics and these nine are cut all at once using a rotary cutter and a plexiglas straight edge.

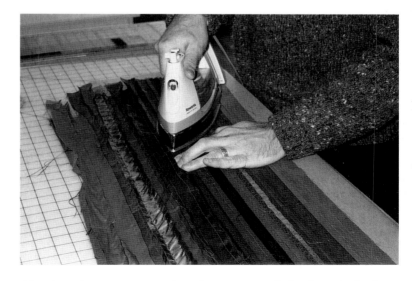

◁ Cut strips are secured together in groups of 36 to await piecing into panels, as time permits.

After the strips are sewn together, they are pressed, first from the back side (leaving seams open) and then from the front.

The collection of some 70 panels, plus fragments and odd pieces, laid out for easy access during construction of the quilt top. These panels are made up of strips that finish at 1″ wide, and are used for larger quilts. The artist also works with an equivalent collection of panels that finish at 3/4″ wide, for use in constructing smaller quilts.

The artist cuts the individual paper forms from the cartoon using a sharp cutter. These forms each serve as pattern pieces for cutting the fabric shapes from the strip-pieced panels.

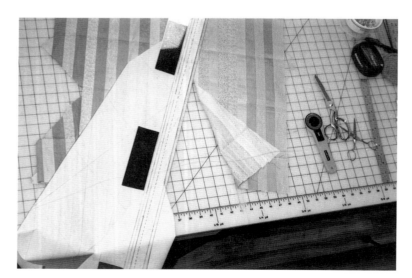

The paper pattern pieces are pinned to the panels and the fabric shapes are cut. The plexiglas ruler is marked with indications for cutting strips of different sizes and also for adding seam allowance where needed, as on this shape.

A full-size cartoon is drafted on large sheets of paper, following the approximate design sketched in the small maquette shown at right. The outlines of all major forms as well as the diagonal strips are indicated.

Along curved edges, seam allowance is added by measuring with a ruler and marking the cutting edge.

Cutting the fabric shape.

The fabric shapes are pinned to the studio wall in the spaces left after removal of the pattern piece from the cartoon.

Pinning of the fabric shapes to the wall allows for ongoing evaluations of the work-in-progress and for frequent changes and alterations that become necessary as new shapes are added and the piece changes and develops.

Once all of the fabric shapes are in place and design problems resolved, the piecing of the top begins, using pins to align seams for precise joints.

As shapes are pieced together, the seams are pressed consistently open.

Piecing a pinned seam.

View in the studio.

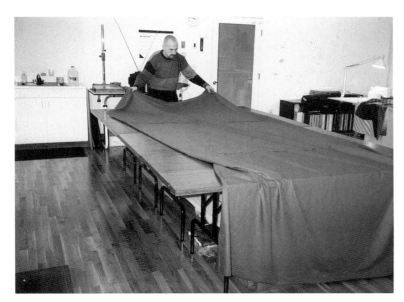

Once the quilt top is completed, the backing fabric is laid out in preparation for securing the three layers of the quilt.

The backing fabric is stretched tightly across the table surface and secured with push pins along its outer sides.

The batting is laid over the backing, followed by the quilt top. The top is smoothed out, and then the seams defining the main forms are adjusted for correct curvature or straightness and pinned through to the backing.

A tailor's basting is used to secure the principal seams so that they will not shift or distort during the quilting process. Basting always takes longer to accomplish than the quilting itself, but the care and attention here is important for accuracy in the final product.

The basted quilt is rolled and the quilting is begun using nylon monofilament as the surface thread and cotton-covered polyester thread in the bobbin. A walking foot is used to prevent creeping of the top layer relative to the backing.

The artist prefers to quilt from the outside edges, moving in to the middle of the piece, because he's learned that this method helps to reduce any distortion in the overall shape of the quilt.

Biography

1949
Born in New Bedford, Massachussetts, June 30. Oldest of seven children of Robert A. James, Jr. and Claire C. (Savoie) James. English and French Canadian heritage.

1954-1967
Elementary and secondary education at St. Anthony's School, New Bedford. At the time, this was a bilingual (French/English) parish school.

1967-1971
Fine art studies at Southeastern Massachussetts University, North Dartmouth. Concentrations in painting and printmaking. Studies color with Donald Kruger.
Initial interest in quilts begins sometime in 1970 with purchase of Dover Books editions of *One Hundred and One Patchwork Patterns* and *The Standard Book of Quiltmaking and Collecting.*

1971
Receives Bachelor of Fine Arts Degree.
Moves to Rochester, New York and begins graduate studies in painting and printmaking at Rochester Institute of Technology. Works principally with non-figurative imagery realized in washes of acrylic stain on unprimed canvas, and multiple print editions in serigraphy. Interest in Native American culture provides a source for visual forms and themes in both paintings and prints.

1972
Marries Judith A. Dionne.
Birth of son, Trevor Dionne James.
Begins making small quilts and patchwork items; largely self-taught.

1973
Receives Master of Fine Arts Degree.
By late summer 1973 has stopped painting in favor of quiltmaking. Does extensive research into quilt history and technique.

1974
In early 1974, attends lecture by Jonathan Holstein at Memorial Art Gallery of the University of Rochester. First exposure to actual Amish quilts.
Moves with his family to Somerset, Massachusetts. Occupies a four-room apartment in which a part of the living room space serves as a studio.

Interweave 7, 1986
60"×60"/152×152 cm

In early autumn begins teaching art part-time at St. Anthony High School in New Bedford, substituting for his former high school art teacher.
Begins teaching adult education workshops in quiltmaking throughout southeastern New England.

1975
While teaching at the DeCordova Museum School, participates in the museum's exhibition *Bed and Board: Quilts and Woodwork,* one of the first large-scale exhibitions featuring non-traditional quilts.
Participates in *Quilts for '76* in the Cyclorama Building of the Boston Center for the Arts.

1976
Attends the first major quilt conference and exhibition held in Ithaca, New York and meets Beth and Jeffrey Gutcheon, Jean Ray Laury, and Myron and Patsy Orlofsky, all leading writers on quilts and quiltmaking.

1977
Begins extensive travels in the U.S. and Canada teaching and lecturing on quiltmaking, quilt design, and historical and contemporary quilts.
First solo exhibition of quilts, at Bridgewater (MA.) State College includes *Night Sky 1, Razzle Dazzle, Elaborated Tangram, and Tossed Salad,* among others.
Night Sky 2 is selected for inclusion in the exhibition *Young Americans: Wood, Plastic, Fiber, Leather* at the Museum of Contemporary Crafts in New York City.
Asked by Prentice-Hall, Inc., of Englewood, New Jersey, through the intermediary of the DeCordova Museum, to write a book on quiltmaking for their Spectrum Books «Creative Handcraft Series».

1978
Participates in the jurying of the first *Quilt National* exhibition in Athens, Ohio. First book, *The Quiltmaker's Handbook: A Guide to Design and Construction,* is published by Prentice-Hall, Inc.
Awarded a Visual Artist Fellowship in Crafts by the National Endowment for the Arts. Begins construction of a home/studio in Somerset Village.

1979
Awarded an Artist's Fellowship by the Boston Artists Foundation. Moves into new home/studio, more than tripling his available workspace.

1980
First trip to England, in May and June, for lecture and workshop tour.

1981

Second book, *The Second Quiltmaker's Handbook: Creative Approaches to Contemporary Quilt Design* is published by Prentice-Hall, Inc.

Completes first corporate commission, *The Seasons*, for the Waltham Federal Savings and Loan Association in Waltham, Massachusetts.

Begins first series of strip-pieced quilts.

1982

Exhibits *Interweave 2* in exhibition *Pattern* at the American Craft Museum, NYC.

1983

First trip to France and Switzerland. Lectures in Paris and in Neuchâtel.

Ten-year retrospective *Michael James: Quiltmaker* takes place in October and November at the Worcester (MA.) Craft Center. Organizes concurrent group exhibition *Fabric Constructions: The Art Quilt* at the Grove Street Gallery in Worcester; it then tours.

1985

Workshop tour in England, Ireland, France and Switzerland. First trip to Italy; visits Venice and Verona.

Travels to Alaska; visits Denali National Park.

Begins *Rhythm/Color* series with *Spanish Dance*, commisioned by the Newark (N.J.) Museum through a grant from the Louis Comfort Tiffany Foundation.

1986

Exhibits *Rhythm/Color: Morris Men* and *Rhythm/Color: Improvisation* in the exhibition *The Art Quilt* at the Los Angeles Municipal Art Gallery. Exhibition tours the U.S.

Participates in the inaugural exhibition of the new American Craft Museum, *Craft Today: Poetry of the Physical*, with *Rhythm/Color: The Concord Cotillion*.

1987

Solo exhibition, *Michael James: New Quilts* takes place at the Wheeler Gallery in Providence, RI. Exhibits *Bias Cut, A View into Time/Motion, Leitmotif*, among others.

1988

Receives a Visual Artists' Fellowship as well as a USA/France Exchange Fellowship from the National Endowment for the Arts.

First European exhibition *Michael James: Nouveaux Quilts* takes place at the Galerie Jonas in Petit Cortaillod, near Neuchâtel, Switzerland. Workshops follow in France, Germany, Holland, and

Switzerland. Spends several days hiking along the Aletsch glacier in south-central Switzerland.

1989

Craft Today USA, organized by the American Craft Museum, begins 3-year European tour at the Musée des Arts Décoratifs du Louvre in Paris. Exhibits *Waves 2*. Begins construction of new studio.

1990

First trip to Japan, at the invitation of Nihon Vogue Company. Ltd. Lectures and workshops in Tokyo and in Osaka. Visits Kyoto.

Completes *Sky/Wind Variations*, a four-part screen commissioned by the Massachusetts Mutual Life Insurance Company in Springfield, MA.

Solo show at Clark University Gallery, Worcester, MA subsequently travels to Galerie Jonas for second European solo exhibition.

Spends three months in artists' residency at the La Napoule Art Foundation at La Napoule, near Cannes, France, with 5 European and 10 American artists. Works on paper exclusively, completing a series of oil pastel drawings.

1991

Begins working in new studio in July.

Aletsch is acquired by the Museum of the American Quilter's Society.

1992

Awared an honorary Doctor of Fine Arts Degree by his alma mater, the University of Massachusetts at Dartmouth (formerly Southeastern Massachusetts University).

1993

Inducted into the Quilter's Hall of Fame, Marion, Indiana.

The Quiltmaker's Handbook and *The Second Quiltmaker's Handbook*, both out-of-print since 1986, are re-published by Leone Publications.

First trips to Florence, Italy and Barcelona, Spain during workshop tour in France and Switzerland.

Waves 2 is acquired by the American Craft Museum, New York, N.Y.

1994

Among four recipients of the first biannual *Society of Arts and Crafts Award* sponsored by the Society of Arts and Crafts of Boston.

Quilt No. 150: Rehoboth Meander is acquired by the Renwick Gallery of the National Museum of American Art of the Smithsonian Institution, Washington, D.C.

Awards

1978
National Endowment for the Arts Fellowship

1979
Boston Artists Foundation Fellowship, Massachusetts

1985
"Fund for the Arts" Grant award for joint exhibition at the Society of Arts and Crafts, Boston, Massachusetts

1988
National Endowment for the Arts Fellowship
Boston Artists' Foundation Fellowship, Massachusetts

1990
USA/France Exchange Fellowship, National Endowment for the Arts and the La Napoule Art Foundation, La Napoule, France; 3 month residency, September to December.

1992
Honorary Doctorate, University of Massachusetts at Dartmouth

1993
Inducted into the Quilter's Hall of Fame, Marion, Indiana

1994
The Society of Arts and Crafts Award, Boston, Massachusetts

One-man Exhibitions

1977
Visual Arts Gallery, Bridgewater State College, Bridgewater, Massachusetts

1978
Visual Arts Gallery, Ohio University, Lancaster, Ohio

1980
LeMoyne Art Foundation, Inc., Tallahassee, Florida

1983
The Worcester Craft Center, Worcester, Massachusetts

1984
Space Gallery, Western Michigan University, Kalamazoo, Michigan

1987
The Wheeler Gallery, Providence, Rhode Island

1988
Galerie Jonas, Petit-Cortaillod, Switzerland

1990
Galerie Jonas, Petit-Cortaillod, Switzerland
Clark University Gallery, Worcester, Massachusetts

1993
Marion Public Library, Marion, Indiana

1995
Galerie Jonas, Petit-Cortaillod, Switzerland

Selected Group Exhibitions

1975
DeCordova Museum, Lincoln, Massachusetts, *Bed and Board*
Boston Center for the Arts, Boston, Massachusetts, *Quilts for '76*

1976
Brockton Art Center, Brockton, Massachusetts, *Craftforms*
Boston City Hall Gallery, Boston, Massachusetts, *Three Centuries of Massachusetts Quilts*

1977
Museum of Contemporary Crafts, New York, New York, *Young Americans: Wood, Plastic, Fiber, Leather*
International Exhibitions Foundation, Washington, DC, *American Quiltmakers*
Society of Arts and Crafts, Boston, Massachusetts, *Show of Hands*
Danforth Library Gallery, New England College, Henniker, New Hampshire, *Third Edition, Ltd.*

1978
Bruce Gallery. Edinboro State College, Edinboro, Pennsylvania, *Intent '78: Fabrics*
Danforth Library Gallery, New England College, Henniker, New Hampshire, *Fourth Edition: New Horizons.*
Brockton Art Center, Brockton, Massachusetts, *The Object: Form Follows Function*
Brockton Art Center, Brockton, Massachusetts, *Hearts and Flowers*
Hunter Museum of Art, Chattanooga, Tennessee, *The Little Quilt*

1979
Worcester Craft Center, Worcester, Massachusetts, *Massachusetts Craftsmen's Fellowship Exhibition*
Stedelijk Museum, Schiedam, Holland, *American Quiltmakers*

1980
American Craft Museum, New York, New York, *Art for Use*

1981
The Dairy Barn Cultural Arts Center, Athens, Ohio, *Quilt National '81*
Kenyon College, Gambier, Ohio, *Contemporary Quilts*
Southern Alleghenies Museum of Art, Loretto, Pennsylvanie, *The New Quilt*

1982
American Craft Museum, New York, New York, *Pattern*

1983
The Dairy Barn Cultural Arts Center, Athens, Ohio, *Quilt National '83*

1984
Musée-Château d'Annecy, Annecy, France and tour *Quilts Contemporains Américains*

Asahi Shimbun and APT, Inc., Tokyo, Japan and tour *Contemporary American Quilts*

1986
American Craft Museum, New York, New York and tour *Craft Today: Poetry of the Physical*
Los Angeles Municipal Art Gallery, California and tour *The Art Quilt*
Society of Arts and Crafts, Boston, Massachusetts, *Constructions (Fund for the Arts Award exhibition)*
University Student Center Gallery, North Carolina State University, Raleigh, North Carolina, *Color: The Spectrum of Expression*

1987
The Dairy Barn Cultural Arts Center, Athens, Ohio, *Quilt National '87*

1989
Musée des Arts Décoratifs du Louvre, Paris, France and tour *Craft Today USA*

1991
Artists Foundation Gallery, Boston, Massachusetts, *Vessels and Textiles: Ancient Forms, New Visions*
The Dairy Barn Cultural Arts Center, Athens, Ohio, *Quilt National '91*
Northern Virginia Fine Arts Association at The Athenaeum, Alexandria, Virginie, *Contemporary Quilts*
Chelsea Gallery, Hinds University Center, Western Carolina University, Cullowhee, North Carolina, *Contemporary Quilts: Seven Innovative Artists*

1992
San Diego Historical Society Museum, California, *Visions: The Art of the Quilt*
The Works Gallery, Philadelphia, Pennsylvania, *Color, Light, and Motion*

1993
University Art Gallery, University of Massachusetts at Dartmouth *Another View: Work by Visiting Artists in Clay, Metal, Wood, Fiber*
Crafts Council, London, England and tour *Contemporary American Quilts*

1994
Society of Arts and Crafts, Boston, Massachusetts, *4 person "Society of Arts and Crafts Award" show*
Kurts Bingham Gallery, Memphis, Tennessee, *Studio Quilts: A Memphis Invitational Exhibition of Contemporary Quilts*

1995
8th Triennial of Tapestry, Central Museum of Textiles, Lodz, Poland

Selected Collections

The Renwick Gallery of the National Museum of American Art, Smithsonian Institution, Washington, D.C.
American Craft Museum, New York, New York
Newark Museum, Newark, New Jersey
Ulster Folk and Transport Museum, Belfast, Northern Ireland
Museum of the American Quilter's Society, Paducah, Kentucky
Ball State University Gallery of Art, Muncie, Indiana
International Business Machines Corporation Essex Junction, Vermont and Marietta, Georgia
Owens-Corning Collection, Owens-Corning Fiberglas Corporation, Toledo, Ohio

American Association of Retired Persons, Washington, D.C.
Massachusetts Mutual Life Insurance Company, Springfield, Massachusetts
Northern Trust Bank, Phoenix, Arizona
Waltham Federal Savings and Loan Association, Waltham, Massachusetts
Nihon Vogue Company, Ltd., Tokyo, Japan
Jack Lenor Larson, New York, New York
The Ardis and Robert James Quilt Collection, Chappaqua, New York

Sky/Wind Variations, 1990
72" × 144" / 183 × 366 cm

Acknowledgements

Artists' careers, and projects such as this monograph that document them, are the work not only of individuals but represent a broader commitment and confidence on the part of the networks of supporters who in various ways help to grow those careers.

Michael James acknowledges his own supporters, and especially: Olivier and Vren Attinger, whose vision and dedication made this volume possible; the National Endowment for the Arts, Washington, D.C., the Massachusetts Council on the Arts and Humanities and the Boston Artists' Foundation, Boston, Massachusetts, the Louis Comfort Tiffany Foundation, New York, N.Y., the La Napoule Art Foundation, New York, N.Y. and La Napoule, France, and the Society of Arts and Craft, Boston, Massachusetts, for financial grants that sustained studio work; numerous public and private collectors, including the Renwick Gallery of the National Museum of American Art of the Smithsonian Institution, Washington, D.C., the American Craft Museum, New York, N.Y., the Newark Museum, Newark, New Jersey, the Museum of the American Quilter's Society, Paducah, Kentucky, the Nihon Vogue Company, Ltd., Tokyo, Japan, the Ulster Folk and Transport Museum, Belfast, Northern Ireland, International Business Machines Corporation, Robert and Ardis James, Philip and Kathy Hess, Brian and Helen White, Rob and Marianne Polak, Alex and Colette Gründisch, Andreas Furrer and Jitka Caslavska, Robert and Helen Millstein, and Joan Kaufmann-Wolfson without whose patronage much less would have been possible; numerous galleries and agents, especially Penny McMorris, Guy and Jacqueline de Montmollin and Galerie Jonas in Petit-Cortaillod, Switzerland, the Works Gallery, Philadelphia, Pennsylvania, the Hand and the Spirit/Joanne Rapp Gallery, Scottsdale, Arizona, and the Kurts Bingham Gallery, Memphis, Tennessee for their efforts in representing the work; the various photographers, especially David Caras, who allowed their images to be reproduced here; Bernina of America, Inc., Aurora, Illinois, the Fairfield Processing Corporation, Danbury, Connecticut, and the Fabric Studio of Swansea, Massachusetts for technical support; many colleagues including Virginia Avery, Pauline Burbidge, Nancy Crow, Nancy Erickson, Jean Ray Laury, Linda MacDonald, Terrie Mangat, Therese May, Risë Nagin, Jan Myers-Newbury, Esther Parkhurst, Barbara Smith and Pamela Studstill for the much-valued stimulation and insights they offer through their own works and through their correspondence; many friends, including Richard and Cynthia Wolbarsht, Charles and Johanna Duponte, Phyllis and Harvey Jeacock, Pamela Hoss, David Hornung, Harry Adler and Laurie Harker, Michele Walker and James Kingston-Stewart, Maryline and Yves Collioud, Jean-Claude and Lucile Moroni, André and Soizik Labbens, Anne Woringer, Ruedi and Ursula König, Hans and Marianne Haeni, Jean-Pierre and Claudine Joho, Karl and Thildi Kellenberger, Olga and Simon Prins, Hildegard Stadler-Götze, Helmut and Erika Odemer, Kei Kobayashi, Mariko Akizuki, Masako and Toshinao Baba, Jim and Catherine Anthony, DeLoris and Herb Stude, Phyllis Weinberg, Joyce Gross, Carolyn Mills, Marjorie and Tom Puryear and Florence Dionne, for their encouragement and more; and the artist's family, especially Judy and Trevor.

Contents

Photo credits

James Beards Photography: pp. 20, 48, 54, 58, 59, 70

David Caras, photographer: jacket, pp. 11, 15, 17, 18, 22, 23, 28, 29, 31, 32, 33, 35, 37, 38, 41, 42, 44, 46, 47, 50, 53, 56, 57, 60, 62, 63, 64, 66, 67, 69, 72, 74, 76, 78, 80, 83, 84, 85, 86, 87, 88, 89

Paul E. Deegan, APSA; MNEC: p. 115

Michael James: pp. 79, 93, 95, 97, 98, 99, 100

JoAnn Sieburg-Baker: pp. 90, 110

Joanne Rapp Gallery/The Hand and the Spirit, Scottsdale: p. 2

Sharon Risedorph: p. 25

Chee-Heng Yeong: p. 6

Printed in Switzerland by Weber Colour Printing Ltd, Bienne

Layout: Olivier Attinger, CH-Chaumont
Typesetting: TransfoTexte, CH-Lausanne
Color-separation: Photolitho Actual, CH-Bienne
Binding: Mayer & Soutter, CH-Lausanne